Comparing **Past** and **Pr**

Going to School

Rebecca Rissman

Heinemann
LIBRARY

Chicago, Illinois

© 2014 Heinemann Library
an imprint of Capstone Global Library, LLC
Chicago, Illinois

To contact Capstone Global Library please phone 800-747-4992, or visit our website www.capstonepub.com

Edited by Rebecca Rissman, Daniel Nunn, and
   Catherine Veitch
Designed by Philippa Jenkins
Picture research by Elizabeth Alexander
Production by Helen McCreath
Originated by Capstone Global Library Ltd

Library of Congress Cataloging-in-Publication Data
Rissman, Rebecca.
  Going to school / Rebecca Rissman.
     pages cm.—(Comparing past and present)
  Includes bibliographical references and index.
  ISBN 978-1-4329-8991-0 (hb)—ISBN 978-1-4329-9025-1
(pb) 1. Schools—History—Juvenile literature. 2. Education—History—Juvenile literature. 3. Educational change—Juvenile literature. I. Title.
  LB1556.R57 2014
  371.009—dc23   2013012542

Image Credits
Alamy: ClassicStock, 10, redsnapper, 7; Getty Images: Brooke, 12, FatCamera, 13, Keystone-France/Gamma Keystone, 6, Kurt Hutton, 14, 18, 23, PhotoAlto/Odilon Dimier, cover (left), Siri Stafford, 11, View Stock, 9; Library of Congress Prints and Photographs: cover (right); Mary Evans Picture Library: 20; Shutterstock: AVAVA, 15, 23, Monkey Business Images, 5, 21, Pressmaster, 17, Zurijeta, 19; Superstock: ClassicStock, back cover, 16, 22, Underwood Photo Archives, 4, 8

We would like to thank Nancy Harris and Diana Bentley for their invaluable help in the preparation of this book.

Every effort has been made to contact copyright holders of material reproduced in this book. Any omissions will be rectified in subsequent printings if notice is given to the publisher.

Contents

Comparing the Past and Present

Things in the past have already happened.

Things in the present are happening now.

Schools have changed over time.

Schools today are very different from schools in the past.

Schools

In the past, most schools were small. Some had only one room!

Today, many schools are very large.

Getting to School

In the past, many children walked a long way to school.

Today, many children ride
in cars or buses to school.

Classes

In the past, children of all ages were in the same class.

Today, most schools place children into different classes by their ages.

School Supplies

In the past, many children wrote on small blackboards.

Today, children write on paper or type on computers.

In the past, schools had few books for children to read.

Today, school libraries have
many books for children to read.

In the past, children learned
things by asking teachers

and reading books.

Today, children can use a computer to learn things. They can also ask teachers and read books.

Lucky Students

In the past, only some lucky children could go to school.

Today, many children can go
to school.

Then and Now

In the past, children enjoyed going to school. Today, children still enjoy school!

Picture Glossary

 **blackboard** dark writing surface. People write with chalk on blackboards.

 **computer** machine that helps people write and learn

Index

Note to Parents and Teachers

Before reading

Talk to children about the differences between the past and present. Explain that things that have already happened are in the past. Ask children to describe their activities from the previous day. Tell children that all of those activities happened in the past. Then explain that the conversation you are having now is happening in the present.

After reading

- Explain to children that the experience of going to school has changed in many ways over time. Ask children to describe their classroom, emphasizing the school materials, class size, and technology. Then ask children to brainstorm about how their experience is different from what children might have experienced in the past.

- Ask children to turn to pages 14—15. Show children the two images, contrasting the technology in modern classrooms with what children used in the past. Then ask children if they can think of any other technology they use at school that did not exist in the past. Keep a record of their ideas on the board, and add any that they might have missed. Remember to include electricity, telephones, and running water.